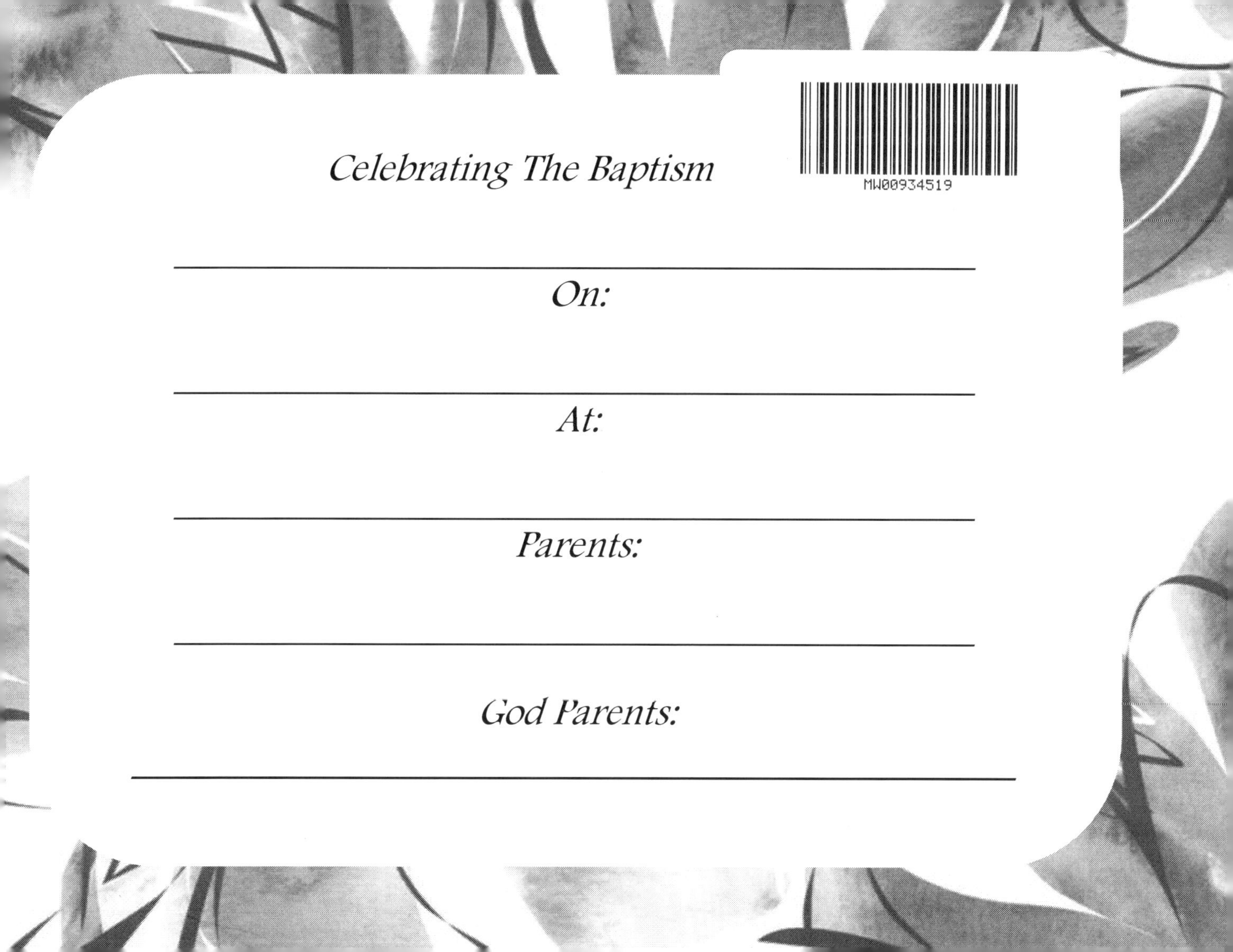
Celebrating The Baptism
MW00934519
On:
At:
Parents:
God Parents:

Bless this little child

Bless
this
little
child

Bless this little child

Bless
this
little
child

Bless this little child

Bless
this
little
child

Bless this little child

Bless
this
little
child

Bless this little child

Bless
this
little
child

Bless this little child

Bless
this
little
child

Bless this little child

Bless
this
little
child

Bless this little child

Bless
this
little
child

Bless this little child

Bless
this
little
child

Bless this little child

Bless
this
little
child

Bless this little child

Bless
this
little
child

Bless this little child

Bless this little child

Bless this little child

Bless
this
little
child

Bless this little child

Bless
this
little
child

Bless this little child

Bless this little child

Bless this little child

Bless
this
little
child

Bless this little child

Bless
this
little
child

Bless this little child

Bless
this
little
child

Bless this little child

Bless
this
little
child

Bless this little child

Bless
this
little
child

Bless this little child

Bless
this
little
child

Bless this little child

Bless
this
little
child

Bless this little child

Bless
this
little
child

Bless this little child

Bless
this
little
child

Bless this little child

Bless
this
little
child

Bless this little child

Bless this little child

Bless this little child

Bless this little child

Bless this little child

Bless this little child

Bless this little child

Bless this little child

Bless this little child

Bless this little child

Bless this little child

Bless this little child

Bless this little child

Bless this little child

Bless this little child

Bless this little child

Bless this little child

Bless this little child

Bless this little child

Bless this little child

Bless this little child

Bless this little child

Bless this little child

Bless this little child

Bless this little child

Bless this little child

Bless this little child

Bless
this
little
child

Bless this little child

Bless this little child

Bless this little child

Bless this little child

Bless this little child

Bless
this
little
child

Bless this little child

Bless this little child

Bless this little child

Bless this little child

Bless this little child

Bless this little child

Gift log

Date	Gift Description	Given By	Thank You Notice Sent

Gift log

Date	Gift Description	Given By	Thank You Notice Sent

Gift log

Date	Gift Description	Given By	Thank You Notice Sent

Gift log

Date	Gift Description	Given By	Thank You Notice Sent

Gift log

Date	Gift Description	Given By	Thank You Notice Sent

Gift log

Date	Gift Description	Given By	Thank You Notice Sent

Gift log

Date	Gift Description	Given By	Thank You Notice Sent

Gift log

Date	Gift Description	Given By	Thank You Notice Sent

Gift log

DATE	GIFT DESCRIPTION	GIVEN BY	THANK YOU NOTICE SENT

Gift log

Date	Gift Description	Given By	Thank You Notice Sent

Made in United States
Orlando, FL
12 May 2022